Joseph Krauskopf

Ninetieth Birthday of Lincoln and Darwin

Joseph Krauskopf

Ninetieth Birthday of Lincoln and Darwin

ISBN/EAN: 9783337197117

Printed in Europe, USA, Canada, Australia, Japan

Cover: Foto ©ninafisch / pixelio.de

More available books at **www.hansebooks.com**

Published Weekly.   Price $1.00 a Year; or Five Cents per copy.

OUR PULPIT.

Sunday Lectures

— OF —

Joseph Krauskopf and J. Leonard Levy.

VOL. XII.   SUNDAY, FEBRUARY 12th, 1899.   No. 18.

Ninetieth Birthday of Lincoln and Darwin

PHILADELPHIA

OSCAR KLONOWER.   1435 EUCLID AVENUE.

Entered at the Post-Office at Philadelphia, as second-class matter.

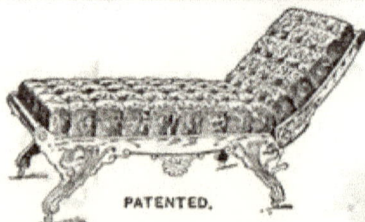

Ninetieth Birthday of Lincoln and Darwin.

A SUNDAY LECTURE

BEFORE THE

REFORM CONGREGATION KENESETH ISRAEL,

BY

RABBI JOS. KRAUSKOPF, D. D.

Philadelphia, February 12th, 1899.

"Emancipators both, Time's twins who taught
The world twin truths long kept from mortal ken :
What *freedom* means at last to freeborn men,
And what the *progress* which our fathers sought."

—FREDERICK LE ROY SARGENT.

Had there really been truth in the former-times pretensions of astrology, and had, ninety years ago this very day, some Nostrodamus been summoned to the town of Shrewsbury on the Severn, to foretell, from the conjunction of the stars, the futurity of the child just born to Dr. Robert Waring Darwin ; and *[The horoscope of twin-born sons of Destiny.]* had, after the horoscope had been cast, the same wizard hastened, by means of his magic art, across the Atlantic, into the wild backwoods region of Kentucky, into the log-cabin of Thomas Lincoln, to prognosticate the fate of the child that had just been born there, he would probably have experienced no little perplexity in the reading of their stars. Amid the greatest possible unlikeness he would probably have traced a strikingly similarity in the destinies of their careers. He would probably have read the signs betokening highest glory for both, yet would have seen these signs overcast by deep shadows, predicting for both labor and trials and martyrdom. To the anxious inquiries of their respective parents he would probably have said : "For mankind's sake, happy the parents who have born them ! For their own sakes, it would have been better, if they had ne'er been born. The world has long had need of them, and yet it will be slow in owning them. It will spurn them long ; it will try them hard, and afflict them sorely, before it will wreathe them with their well-deserved laurels, before it will recognize their distinguished services, and do them homage."

It is difficult to ponder on the lives of both these mighty men of genius, Abraham Lincoln and Charles Darwin, both born on the same day of the same month of the same year, both, though thousands of miles apart, consecrating themselves, at the same time, silently and unweariedly, for a like great mission ; *[Their likeness seemingly of higher decree.]* both, though unknown to each other, bursting, at the very same time, into the public arena as mighty emancipators, the one of thought, the other of people ; both drawing down upon themselves, at the very same time, their fellowmen's wrath and fury for their heroic daring ; both classed alike to-day with the world's greatest benefactors :—it is difficult to ponder on the marvellous likeness of careers of these otherwise most unlike men, and not feel that there was a divine purpose in their common birthdays, and that a like divinity shaped even their very unlikenesses for like blessed ends.

It was the atmosphere of a home of wealth, of cultured surroundings, of intellectual associationship that Darwin needed for the nurture of great mind. It was the atmosphere of the wretched log-cabin, and the environment of unlettered people, and of unbridled elements and untamed forces that Lincoln required for the nurture of sinewy manhood and of heroic endurance. The sphere cf the life-work of the one was to lie in the retreats of nature, and in the seclusion of laboratories and libraries ; that of the other was destined to be out in the world, and among the people, and among the very lowest of them as well as among the very highest. The one needed the ease and opulence so essential for quiet study and patient research and costly experimentation, for he was destined to wage the battle of books against the pretensions of ignorance, and to employ the skill of profound erudition, and to wield as weapons the unconquerable logic of observed and experimented fact. The other required hardship and privation, for his was to be a battle, long and fierce, against deep-rooted prejudices and bitter hatreds and intense passions, in which the skill acquired in the bitter school of adversity, and the knowledge gotten through contact with all sorts and conditions of men, can alone hope for ultimate success. And destiny seemed to have taken precautionary measures, in time, to enforce its wish, for the one it endowed with a delicate constitution, and with a shy and reticent nature, to necessitate his retired life within his study and laboratory ; while to the other it gave the physical strength of the giant, and the boldness of the lion, to enforce his entrance into the world, and to enable him to challenge some of its wrongs to mortal combat, and conquer them.

And so we find Charles Darwin given very early in life an opportunity for developing his intellectual endowments, which, to a considerable extent, heredity had made his birthright. He was sent to the very best school in town, where even as a boy he began to show that love of collecting plants and minerals and insects, that constituted the ruling passion of his life, but which did by no means meet with the approval of his teachers. Because he preferred living nature to the dead languages, which constituted then almost all the subjects that were taught, and in which he could neither find nor take any interest, he was generally considered as neither bright nor promising, so much so that his father said to him one day, in a spirit of distemper, " You care for nothing but shooting, dogs, and rat-catching, and you will be a disgrace to yourself and all your family." When about that time an opportunity was afforded him for the study of Chemistry, he evinced such a zeal, especially in his experimentation with gases and their compounds, that he brought down upon himself the nick-name of "Gas," and the public rebuke by the Head-Master of the school for wasting his time on utterly useless subjects.

At the age of fifteen, he matriculated in Scotland's greatest seat of learning, the University of Edinburgh, to prepare himself there for the medical profession, in which his father had built up a very large and a very lucrative practice. But even the medical profession was not to young Darwin's taste, and the father, recognizing it at last, after two years of wasted time, sent him to the University of Cambridge, to fit himself there for the ministry. Think of him, who has been attacked more bitterly than any other scientist as an enemy to religion, fitting himself for three long years for the life of a clergyman! He worked hard during that period, even in the dead languages and still deader theologies, to refute his father's angry predictions that he would turn out an idle sporting man. But try as he would, theology was as little to his taste as medicine had been. His nature could not be bound to any profession. He preferred the living book of Nature, to the dead systems of theology. Nature alone had the intensest interest for him ; within it he lived ; there he worshipped ; to it he was devoted with a zeal, of which the following incident, related by himself, may serve as an example : "One day, on tearing off some old bark, I saw two rare beetles, and seized one in each hand ; then I saw a third and new kind, which I could not bear to lose, so that I popped the one which I held in my right hand into my mouth. Alas ! it ejected some intensely acrid fluid, which burnt my tongue so that I was forced to spit the beetle out, which was lost, as was the third one."

A passion for Natural History as intense as this convinced his father at last that when Destiny calls one of the sons of men into a special field, and for a special work, neither father nor teacher nor school, and be they never so self-willed or learned or so famed, can thwart her. What she wills, will be. Deeper and deeper his soul rooted itself in Science. Wider and wider grew his acquaintanceship with scientific men and scientific literature. Greater and greater grew his indifference to theology as a profession. The decisive hour came at last. The *Beagle* was about to start for the Tropics on a surveying expedition for the Government. A naturalist was wanted by the Lords of the Admiralty to accompany it. Young Darwin was recommended for it by one of the University Professors. His father opposed his going. "If you can find any man of common sense," said he, "who advises you to go, I will give my consent." That common-sense adviser was speedily found, and forth he sailed on a journey of research that lasted five years, and of which he said that it proved by far the most important event in his life, and determined his whole career.

The will of Destiny cannot be thwarted.

Let us leave our young scientific enthusiast in yonder Southern seas, and let us turn to our own Southern borders, to the wilds of Kentucky of

4

Lincoln's primitive childhood's surroundings. ninety years ago, and follow the early struggles of that other hero, whose birthday we likewise commemorate to-day. What a change from the surroundings in which we saw Darwin pass his childhood and youth! Instead of the high state of culture, which we found within his home, and within the school of his native town, and within the chief Universities of Scotland and England, we find Lincoln passing the first score years of his life among frightfully primitive surroundings. The country is wild, uncleared, save a few patches from which the poor settlers coax a pitiable living. The homes are wretched log-cabins, for the most part without floors, doors, windows and chimneys. A few boards and planks and sticks constitute their furniture, and a few earthen and pewter pots and pans make up all their kitchen utensils. On the one side, the few domestic animals are housed ; the other side serves as the family's kitchen and dining-room, and sleeping apartment and parlor, all in one. The people's attire is coarse and unsightly, largely made by unskilled hands from skins and furs of wild animals, which their rifles had brought down. Their food is of the commonest, little better than that which is fed to the cattle ; even the potato is a delicacy to be indulged in only on special occasions, and only by the few well-to-do. The culture of the people is in keeping with their surroundings, their manners are rough, their habits coarse, drinking and fighting are common, even among the women. Of education there is little that can pass by that name ; the men and women able to write are very few ; books are fewer ; teachers and schools fewer still.

Within such surroundings stood Lincoln's cradle, if such a piece of furniture as a cradle was ever known in these wilds of Kentucky, ninety years ago. His father was a backwoodsman in the fullest His boyhood's struggles and privations. sense of the word, unmannered, unlettered, thriftless, shiftless. His mother, Nancy Hanks, was a frail and delicate creature, who, under more favorable environments and within easier conditions, might have blossomed into a woman of considerable strength and culture. Slowly she pined away, and finally died, before her little Abe had reached his ninth year, and before she had succeeded in teaching him more than his letters and a little spelling.

We next see the family, forced by the direst necessity, changing its location from Kentucky to Indiana. Even here existence continued to be a keen struggle. Yet the environments were not quite as primitive as in Kentucky, and the chances for a littte education were a trifle better, and young Lincoln was not the lad to let such an opportunity pass, small as it was. Here he obtained his first schooling, and his last, seven months in all, in all his life, within a school located in a log-cabin, four miles away, and to which the boy had to trudge, in all sorts of weather, whenever his father could spare him from his carpentering and farming and rail-splitting work, which was not any too often. Poor lad, how hard he had to labor in those days to satisfy the needs of his family, and how much harder still to satisfy the hunger and thirst of his mind for knowledge. They called him lazy, and some believed him daft, when they saw him lying flat under the trees or in front of the chimney fire during the few leisure hours that were his, poring over the four or five books that constituted his whole library, or when they watched him using, for the want of slate or paper, the broad surface of his wooden shovel, or the flat side of logs, when practicing the art of writing and figuring or when noting down his thoughts and impressions. But what mattered their jeering to him. His mind had fully awakened; it had experienced its first sunrise; the deep darkness had disappeared; his soul had received its first bath in the roseate light of the intellectual dawn. Borne upwards on the pinions of light and hope, his spirit soared far beyond his mean and poverty-stricken surroundings. Even while he labored, he sought and found knowledge, and when the book failed him originality stepped in, and where the printed text was wanting memory supplied. A great original character was slowly unfolding itself there in the forest land of Indiana, and all his physical hardships and all his intellectual struggles were but tributary to its moulding.

'Let us cease our musings, and hastily follow his gradual rise from these untoward conditions to the very forefront of the Nation. When about of age, the family, for the second time, changes its place of habitation, this time to Illinois. Conditions here are somewhat more favorable, and afford the young struggler a few opportunities in the way of self-education *Receives his first divine inspiration and commission.* that had been denied him before. One of these is destined to prove the turning-point of his life, and to shape his whole life's mission. He accompanies, as a hired hand, a flat-boat laden with provisions down to New Orleans. For the first time in his life he catches a glimpse of the world, and of the vastness of his native land, and of the extent of the horror of his nation's curse, the curse of slavery. There, in the slave-mart, he sees human beings sold like cattle, husbands and wives, parents and children, brothers and sisters, torn from each other, their pitiful cries and heart-rendering shrieks awakening no pang of conscience, no spark of 'sympathy in the hearts of purchasers. Lincoln looks on amazed and bitterly aggrieved. Around him he hears the heartless commands and the insulting jests of cruel overseers. His righteous passions are all aflame. His soul receives its first inspiration. Turning to his companion he says " John, if I ever get a chance to hit that institution, I'll hit it hard, by the Eternal God !"

To hit the accursed institution of slavery, and to hit it hard, obviously required two prerequisites, first, the courage of fighting, secondly, the knowledge how. And so we find him, shortly after his return from the southern slave-state, serving as a captain in the war against the Black Hawk Indians, and, *Chosen for the crown of thorns.* then, after peace is restored, commencing the study of law, supporting himself in the meantime as a clerk of a grocery store, of a postoffice, of a surveying-office. We next see him entering the political arena, and it is not long before, as Holland informs us, we find him shouldering his pack and trudging on foot to Vandalia, then the Capital of the State, about a hundred miles, to make his entrance into public life as a State Legislator, and to take his stand soon after as a bitter opponent to the spread of slavery. The die is cast ; he has taken the stand that is to make him the greatest master and greatest martyr of the Nation. It is not long before it hurries him to the Capital of the Nation, as a representative of his State in Congress. It summons him home again to fight the cause of slavery with the keenest weapons of logic that have ever been wielded in any cause, against his great opponent, Stephen A. Douglas, by far the ablest of Northern Democratic politicians. With bated breath the whole nation watches these battles of the giants. It marvels at the profound grasp of the subject of slavery, and at its powerful presentation by that tall, lank, ungainly, ill-dressed, self-reared, self-taught orator and statesman of the West. The long looked-for leader against the no longer suppressible crisis had made his appearance. The Messiah was born. The Redeemer had come. The ear attuned to celestial music could distinctly hear the angel choral : " Glory to God on highest, on earth peace, good will toward all men." In a happy hour for itself, and for three millions of fettered slaves, but in an unfortunate hour for himself, the Nation chose him for its President.

While he is getting himself ready for his crown of thorns, let us hasten across the ocean to catch a glimpse of that other son of Destiny,

His twin-brother, Darwin, at the same time, attracts world's attention. who, at the very same time, is dividing the world's attention with his American twin-brother. With a suddenness, equal to that of Lincoln, Charles Darwin had stepped to the very forefront of the world of science. After spending five years in researches within the tropics, and after devoting twenty years to investigations in the seclusion of his study and laboratories and greenhouses, he had came out with his epoch-making book *The Origin of Species*. The world of science held its breath; the world of theology was stunned. And when both recovered from their first shock, there was an outcry the like of which had never been heard before. The one denounced it as a Revolution; the other branded it a Rebellion, the rest of the reading world ranged itself partly on the one side, and partly on the other, and the war was on, and in bitter earnest.

Some of us wonder to-day what there was in Darwin's teaching so terrible to have evoked that world-wide storm of wrath and fury. We

His epoch-making discovery denounced as atheism. forget that what to-day is almost school-boy knowledge, a commonplace in the scientific laboratories, was unheard of, undreamed of, two score years ago. Who had heard, upon the authority of empirical science, that the Biblical teaching respecting the origin of the universe, namely, that it had been called forth some six thousand years ago, in six successive days, by means of six successive Divine utterances, was no longer tenable in the light of modern researches? Who had heard of so strange a doctrine that the universe, as we now see it, is the result of an exceedingly slow evolution that has been in progress for countless millions of years, that all that exists has passed through gradual changes and unfoldings from the lowest to the highest, from the simplest to the most complex, from nebula to constellation, from lichen to palm, from germ-cell to man? There was no abuse so cruel which they did not heap upon him; no accusation so false which they did not charge him with. Men who never read his work, would not read it, could not read it, denounced him bitterest. Preachers, who had not one-half the piety he had, who knew not one-hundredth part of the wonders and mysteries of God's handiwork that he did, branded him from pulpit, platform and in press, as an atheist, as in league with Satan against God, and warned their flocks for their soul's salvation sake, against the reading of the book, whose letters exuded a poison more fatal than that of the most poisonous serpent. To call a man a *Darwinian* was with one fell blow to exclude him from the church and from decent society. Even scientists of distinctions for a long time joined in this fierce crusade against the author, who had so grievously sinned against God and man by daring to give to the world the results of almost half a century's patient and laborious researches, and observed and experimented facts, who, by affording the mind an intelligent insight into the laboratory of nature, in which God designs and executes his wondrous work, broke its bonds of dogmatic slavery, emancipated it from the thraldom of theological tyranny, freed it from the oppressive shackles of primitive myths and speculations.

But our hero labored on. He felt the injustice and the cruelty of the charges keenly, yet continued he silently and labored on. Truth he knew would conquer, in spite of anathemas and maledictions by prelate or bishop or dean, by scientist or sciolist or ignoramus. Gradually the world's best thought veered toward him. Abuse lessened; admiration increased. Men *The crown of thorns changes into a crown of glory for Darwin.* began to read without prejudice, and began to recognize more clearly than they ever had in the creation-story of the Bible, the wondrous creation of the Divine Creator, which Darwin had interpreted in the devout language of science, and whose Author he had revealed in the spirit of the Sage. Work followed upon work, and admiration heightened to veneration. Universities and learned societies all over the world, vied with one another in conferring honors and degrees and medals upon him. And when at last, his three score years and ten having been passed, he laid down his pen to take his final rest, his Nation would not have it otherwise but that he must be buried in the consecrated and coveted ground of Westminster Abbey, with its most celebrated men paying the Nation's last tribute of respect as pall-bearers.

We shall not wait to listen to the eloquent eulogies that are spoken, but hasten across the Atlantic to his American twin-brother, who when last we saw him, twenty-two years before the death of Darwin, was getting himself ready for the crown of thorns. We find him back again in the Capital of Illinois, likewise *Into a halo of martyrdom for Lincoln.* sleeping his eternal sleep, and within a monumental tomb, the proud tribute of his Nation. And the story of his brief but troubled yet blessed reign is told us, and it is difficult to believe that it is not to some ancient chronicle of martyrology that we listen, so full of suffering, so marvellous in achievement, so horrible in martyrdom. He was stricken dead by the assassin's hand, but not before he had dealt slavery its death-blow. He had proved himself the Suffering Messiah, the Vicarious Atonement. He had died the Death of a Redeemer, on the "Good Friday," April 14th, of 1865. He had gotten the chance to hit trafficking with human flesh a hard blow, and three millions of emancipated negroes, and a whole Nation federated in peaceful union, testify how hard he hit it.

Never was tragedy written so thrilling as that story of those five years that intervene between his preparing himself for the crown of thorns and

The five years passion of the Redeemer.

his returning encircled with the halo of martyrdom; his stealing into Washington to escape assassination; his fearless utterances in his inaugural address, utterances, which, though they ultimately saved the Union, and freed the slave, found their response in the firing upon Fort Sumter, in the secession of the Southern States, and in one of the bloodiest Civil Wars that has ever been waged; his cabinet's distrust of him; the leaders' lack of confidence in his ability to lead the Nation to victory through so great a crisis and so fierce a struggle; the abolitionist's impatience with him for moving so slowly; the conservatives' desertion of him for moving so fast; the Anti Slavery party's denunciation of him for making the Union his chief concern; the Unionist's abandonment of him for giving the slave question undue prominence; his standing almost all alone, hated, reviled, despised, lampooned, ridiculed, defied, plotted against, held responsible for every defeat on battlefield or at election-poll; every military blunder, every miscarriage of political plan, laid at his door, standing there, all alone, like a towering light-house in a sea of trouble, with the warring billows raging below, with the angry skies hurling death and destruction from above, oh, it is a tragedy terrible, yet sublime, a theme heroic for a far more gifted tongue than mine, for a far abler pen than I have at my command.

Firm he stood, immoveable as the eternal rock, his goal all the clearer in front of him, and all the surer and faster approached the bitterer the

The Redeemer glorified.

opposition, the fiercer the attack. Self-interest had no weight with him,—what of it if he suffer, if but the slave is free! What of it if he die, if but the Union lives! What of it if he be cursed, if but the Nation is freed from the curse of slavery! What of it if he be the condemned of people, if but his course is approved by his conscience and by the Eternal God!

And what he suffered for, and what he died for, that has he achieved. The Union lives; the Slave is free; the Nation is cleansed of the stain of centuries. He, that was the accursed of the people, has become the Nation's Saint, its greatest Master, its holiest Martyr, a people's Messiah and Redeemer, the Talisman and Patron forever of every tyrannized people, of every down-trodden, God-given right.

MORTUARY CHAMBER AND CHAPEL AT MOUNT SINAI CEMETERY.

Our ❧ ❧ Pulpit ❧

Published Weekly

Price $1.00 a Year
or
Five Cents per copy

Sunday Discourses

of

Rabbi JOSEPH KRAUSKOPF, D. D.

VOL. XVIII.   Sunday, February 12th, 1905.   No. 14.

Lincoln—an Inspiration.

PHILADELPHIA

OSCAR KLONOWER   1435 EUCLID AVENUE

Lincoln—an Inspiration.

A Discourse, at Temple Keneseth Israel,

BY

Rabbi Joseph Krauskopf, D. D.

Philadelphia, February 12th, 1905.

Scriptural Lesson   I Samuel, Chapter XVI, 1–13.

Text : "Who shall stand in the holy place? He that hath clean hands, and a pure heart." Psalm XXIV, 3–4.

Mr. William Roscoe Thayer contributes to the current number of the *North American Review* a scholarly article, entitled : Biography. In it he sets forth that biography as a branch of history is little culti- *The worth of biography.* vated, and that of good biographies we have but few. He tells us that, if Plutarch's Lives had been lost, we would have been deprived of knowledge such as neither Thucydides nor Livy nor Tacitus could ever supply. He attributes the never-weakening hold of the Old Testament on civilized society not so much to its religious as to its biographical teaching. Abraham, Isaac, Joseph, Moses, Saul, David, and others, are drawn, he says, with such unsurpassed fidelity that a child recognizes the life-likeness, and a philosopher wonders at the perfection with which they typify phases of universal human nature. He shows that the nineteenth century produced Lives as great as any that lived in times past, and some types greater than any that had ever been recorded before, but they have largely escaped us because of our disregard of biography as one of the most important branches of knowledge. In this age of science, he says, it is the mass or the class that holds our attention ; of the individual little account is taken. "The career of a tribe, a nation, a race; the growth and decay of institutions; the birth and flowering and death of religions, philosophies, politics, arts; the mystic importance of the soil out of which all springs, and of the climate which each must breathe—these are the topics," he says, "which have chiefly engrossed historians during the past fifty years." The conclusion arrived at is that man's highest interest is in his fellowman, and that the knowledge of other men's lives is the secret of knowing how best to live one's own.

I wish that educators and parents might read that article, and be inspired by it to attach greater importance to biography than they have hitherto in the training of those who are entrusted to their care. And I wish that the Nation would make a study of the lives of its great and good men and women obligatory in all its schools, to assure itself thereby of a nobler type of manhood and of a higher grade of citizenship. I believe that one of the curses of our age is to be found in the preponderating publication by our press of what is vicious and criminal, in the conspicuous exhibition of ignoble types of character, of corrupt politicians, of apathetic citizens, of scoundrelism in high life and low life. The constant sight and sound of these evils, unneutralized by an occasional dipping into the lives of the Nation's noblest heroes and martyrs, diseases our moral nature, as the constant in-breathing of noxious gases poisons our physical health. Unconsciously, a belief implants itself that all are grasping and self-seeking, that all set their own gain above that of the state—that no one is capable of self-sacrifice for his country's good, and that, when all politicians are dishonest and all citizens apathetic, no one but a fool will be honest if in office, and no one but an idler will bother himself about national or municipal affairs, if out of office.

It is to this absence of noble types of patriots as exemplars by which to guide our political lives, it is to this want of hero-worship which manifests itself best in love of biography, that I attribute the little importance that is attached to this day, which is known in our national calendar as *Lincoln's Birthday*.

What if Lincoln had lived in ancient days, and had performed his valorous deeds and had suffered martyrdom in Biblical times! What a joyous religious festival we would have celebrated to-day! How the church-bells would have summoned the people to their respective place of worship! How the sacred edifices would have

Its study should be obligatory in all schools.

Its neglect accounts for neglect of Lincoln's birthday.

What if Lincoln had been a Biblical character?

been garlanded and festooned in honor of the patriot, hero and martyr! How the pulpits would have waxed eloquent in their recitals of his heroic and beneficent achievements! How augmented choirs and crowded congregations would have made the churches reverberate with their pæans of triumph, with their hymns of praise!

Secular institutions are not generally willing to learn from the church; whether with good reason or not is not for me to tell. But I cannot help thinking that they might Secular institu-profitably copy from the church its mode of cele- tions might profit brating the anniversaries of its saints and heroes, from church. its mode of devoting lesson, discourse and hymn to the story of their lives and deeds. They would find it one of the noblest manners of commemorating the dead, and one of the best means of inspiring the living.

As there is little likelihood of secular institutions following this example of the church, why might not the church make festive days of the anniversaries of its national Church should heroes and martyrs? Must the church confine celebrate secular itself for its anniversary celebrations only to saints benefactors. and heroes who lived thousands of years ago, or who were of Palestinian or Roman origin? Did the great benefactors of mankind live only in ancient times? Have not modern times seen reformers, emancipators, benefactors, martyrs, holy men and holy women, saints in the truest sense of the word, as great as any of those who lived in the past? Why are not they given a place in the calendar of the church? Was not their cause God's cause, their battle God's battle, their victory God's victory? Did not they sow in tears that mankind might reap in joy? Did not they pour out their heart's blood that their nations might live in peace and happiness?

Often I feel that the church, by refusing to take cogniz-ance of modern benefactors, is losing sight of one of the greatest opportunities for impressing itself strongly upon Lincoln as great as the present generation. Such recognition of dis- greatest of ancient tinguished and heroic benefaction would give heroes. modern interest to the church, and enhance its worth as an educator and inspirer. If the story of Moses emancipating an oppressed people more than three thousand years ago, or that of a Maccabee taking up, in the name of liberty, an almost lost cause, and routing a mighty host, can thrill and inspire us to-day, how might we not be thrilled and inspired by a church celebration of Abraham Lincoln, the lowly and despised, yet the God-inspired and fearless, setting free three millions of enslaved human beings, and securing the permanence of our Nation, at the cost of his life !

The Catholic Church has been wiser in this respect than we. It did not cease celebrating and sanctifying men and women with the close of its Scripture. It has **Lincoln deserving of canonization.** gone on canonizing people who powerfully impressed their personality on contemporaneous and succeeding generations. It erred, however, in limiting that distinction to people of its own faith, and to such who benefitted its church. Its roster of saints does not contain the names of the men and women of the larger faith, of the faith as broad as human kind, of them who fought mankind's battles, who healed mankind's wounds, who broke the shackles of the enslaved, who fought and bled and died for liberty, justice and truth, the Charlotte Cordays, the Lessings, the Florence Nightingales, the John Howards, the Father Damiens, the Garrisons, the Lincolns.

Name the *saints' days* of all the churches, and tell a prouder day than February, the twelfth. Enumerate all the valorous deeds of all the holy men, and tell me **What saint greater than Lincoln?** which will eclipse those of Abraham Lincoln. Tell the story of the brightest star in your galaxy of saints, of one who, rising from lowliest origin, of one who, unaided by any of the advantages of education or culture or good family, or good looks or social graces, of one who, entirely self-taught and self-trained, of one who, obliged to fight all his life against adverse circumstances, of one who with a world against him, and with no other weapon than an unquenchable love for right and justice, and with an immovable conviction that truth will be, must be victorious in the end, dared all and conquered all, and when you have told that story, compare it with that of Abraham Lincoln, and then tell me which is the more illustrious, which the more inspiring of the two.

There has never lived a saint, though their name is Legion, whose life and deeds have so kindled a love of true heroism in the heart of the reader as does the story of the life of Lincoln. It is almost im- His life an inspiration. possible for you to rise from the reading of his biography, and not have a more sacred regard for the possibilities of true manhood than you ever had before, and not have a new light in your eye, a new love in your heart, a new purpose to your life, a new resolve: so to live, henceforth, and so to strive that mankind may, in some measure, be the better for your living. It is for this reason that I believe that the church would render one of the greatest services to mankind if it would gather its people together every twelfth of February, for a sacred commemoration of the heroic part Lincoln played in one of the world's bitterest struggles and proudest victories. No one could attend that service and not go away the wiser and better for having come and listened to a story which, without the aid of myth and miracle, without the halo of exaggeration and embellishment, is stranger than fiction, and more marvellous than legend born of oriental fancy.

There are times when nations, like individuals, perform master-strokes of genius. Such a one was performed by our Nation on that day—one of the most critical in His choice a its history—when it dared to choose one, unknown master-stroke of to most, scorned by many, doubted by the best, genius. yet destined, before long, to win the admiration of all, and to grow deeper into the heart of the American than has any other President, before or since. And it was no special manifestation of divine aid, no supernatural power to work miracles or to cast spells that opened to him the heart of men, that made him the redeemer of the oppressed, the savior of his people.

No man ever had a more difficult path to travel than he, and had he lived in the days when the supernatural had general credence, when it was commonly resorted No man climbed to explain what otherwise seemed inexplicable, a more difficult a dozen miracles would have been invented for height. him by his admirers, a dozen revelations would have been vouchsafed for him by his chroniclers, to account for his march from his log-cabin in the wilds of Kentucky to the White House at Washington.

No President before or since had been the object of as much vilification, ridicule, carricature as he had been during the short tenure of his office. That which was his glory was made his shame; that wherein lay his greatness was held up as his disgrace; that which was his highest wisdom was ridiculed as his monumental folly. Yet, when he was foully felled by the hand of felon, in the very hour of his supremest triumph, the whole Nation wept; the sun and moon seemed to have lost their lustre; the birds in the air seemed to have hushed their voices; the stars and stripes of Old Glory seemed to have paled and shrunken; Jefferson Davis, the leader of the rebellion, mourned the dastardly deed as the greatest calamity to the South next to the failure of the confederacy; and all the nations of the earth vied with each other in doing reverence to his memory, and in sympathizing with the Nation for its irreparable loss.

From most abused becomes most honored.

What was the miracle that wrought the mighty change within so short a time?

It was first of all the simplicity of his nature. His was a mind as open as the woodland in which he was raised; his a soul as clear and sunny as the sky under which he was born. A commoner by birth, a commoner he remained all his life. Honors could never spoil him; position could never make him forget his worse than humble birth—a childhood with little of a mother's care or of a father's guidance, with scarcely any schooling, with but few books, few friends, few of those pleasures that make childhood a happy memory. He never tried, not even when in the zenith of his glory, to assume a polish or grace or manner that was not his by nature or training. This plainness it was that kept him close to the great majority of the people whose kinsman he was by birth and fortune. Being of the common people, he knew their wants, he had his ear close to their hearts, and when he said and did a thing it was the utterance or the deed of the people incarnate in himself. What a beautiful saying that was of his "God must love the common people, or He would not have made so many of them." What a flash of genius in that answer of his, to the question what his coat of arms would be, "A pair of shirt-sleeves."

Change of sentiment due to his simplicity.

The second cause that wrought that miracle lay in his sterling honesty. Other men have risen from lowly estates to positions of eminence, but seldom with the aid of such uncompromising integrity as that which distinguished the life of Lincoln. Enemies derided, newspapers carricatured him, but no one could ever point a finger of calumny at his honor or honesty. Almost unlimited was the power he possessed, vast was the national treasure under his administration, yet no one was ever able to say that he used his power for personal glory or disposed of treasure for personal ends. No one was ever able to charge him with consulting any other interests than those of his country, or with seeking any other welfare than that of his people. His very face disarmed suspicion. He had never mingled enough with society to have learned the art of posing or dissembling. His greatness lay in his goodness.

To his sterling honesty.

Remarkable as was the power with which he could bear abuse, his ability to forgive was more remarkable still. That beautiful saying of his in his inaugural address: " With malice toward none, with charity toward all " was the guiding principle of his entire public career, and often under most trying and vexing conditions. He could afford to be honest because he never sought an honor and was never ruled by ambition. Whatever office he held sought him; whatever honor he had came unsolicited. When advised one day by friends to change a certain expression in an address he was about to deliver, lest it might lose him votes and lead to his defeat, he replied that that expression was his matured conviction, that it was the truth and the whole truth, and that he could better afford defeat with that expression than victory without it.

It was in that sacred regard for right wherein lay another cause of that marvellous change in the attitude of the Nation toward one whom, but a short time before the leaders scorned or distrusted, or whose ability to lead the Nation through one of the greatest crises even his friends seriously questioned. He had seen slavery in all its sinfulness, and he had sworn to himself that, if ever he should have the power, he would, with God's aid, give it the blow that would crush it forever. He never forgot

To his sacred regard for right.

that pledge. "There is but one question before the American people," said he, early in his career. "'Is Slavery Right or Wrong?' and until that question is answered peace is impossible, and the Union is in danger." And all fearless of the consequences to his political opportunities, he continued, saying: "You cannot, you dare not say that slavery is right! Have the manhood then to say 'it is wrong,' and the courage to stand by your conviction. History, through the centuries, has been teaching us that might ma es right! Let it be our mission in this nineteenth century to reverse the maxim and to declare that right makes might!"

They who were present at that speech saw his face, that at other times was almost ugly, made beautiful by the ecstasy of his wrath, saw his stature, already six feet and four inches in height, grow into colossal proportions, and in his voice they heard the ring that must have been heard at Pharaoh's court, when Moses thundered forth: "Let my people free!" or that must have been heard at the Diet of Worms, when Luther, in the face of death, gave utterance to his declaration of conviction: "Here I stand, I cannot otherwise, God help me. Amen."

Verily as a messenger of God spoke Lincoln on that day, and if his hearers did not know it at the beginning of his address, all doubt was dispelled when he concluded that memorable speech with the words: "I know that the Lord is always on the side of the right; but it is my constant anxiety and prayer that I and this Nation should be on the Lord's side."

If men have been called saints because of the holiness of their lives, then is our own Lincoln entitled to saintship. If men A saint and seer, have been called prophets because of the lumia reformer and nous truths they uttered, because of their fearless an emancipator. exposure of wrong, and their defense of right, because of their clear prevision of the consequences of wrong, and their heroic efforts to ward them off by converting error into truth, and iniquity into righteousness, then was Lincoln a prophet. If men have been called reformers and emancipators for abolishing the wrongs of ages and for setting free the oppressed and the enslaved, then was Lincoln a reformer and an emancipator. If men have been called martyrs for purchasing other men's rights, and other men's freedom, and other men's happiness at the cost of their own lives, then died Lincoln the death of martyrdom.

And if for these reasons, the saints and prophets, the reformers and emancipators and martyrs, have found a place in the memorial calendar of the church, then is Lincoln entitled to a foremost place among the sainted and blessed of every church, for a better man than he, nor one greater, nor one more blessed than he never lived in any age, nor in any clime.

Our · · **Pulpit** ·

Published Weekly

Price $1.00 a Year
or
Five Cents per copy

Sunday Discourses

of

Rabbi JOSEPH KRAUSKOPF, D. D.

VOL. XIX.   Sunday, February 11th, 1906.   No. 15.

Lincoln, the Chosen of God

The Discourse No. 14, delivered Sunday, Feb. 4th,

The Poverty of the Rich,

will appear in our next issue.

PHILADELPHIA

OSCAR KLONOWER   1435 EUCLID AVENUE

Entered at the Post-Office at Philadelphia, as second-class matter.

The following Lectures of Rabbi Jos. Krauskopf, D. D. can be had on receipt of price.—5c. per copy—from Oscar Klonower, 1435 Euclid Ave., Phila., Pa.

SERIES I. 1887—1888.

14. The Hebrew and the Atheist.
16. Passover and Easter.
18. Who is Responsible (The State).
20. The Saturday and Sunday Sabbath.

SERIES II. 1888—1889.

9. The Ideal Commonwealth.
10. The Puritanic Sabbath.
13. The Messianic Age.
23. The 25th Anniversary of Corner Stone of K. I.
25. A Benefactor Honored (Rev. Dr. Wise).
27. The Removal of the Leaven.
25. Deed Through Creed.

SERIES III. 1889—1890.

6. A Child's Prayer.
9. Are We Better than the Heathen?
16. Myths in the New Testament.
20. Purim and Lent.
23. War Against War.
24. Martyr's Day.
26. Ancient and Modern Saints.

SERIES IV. 1890—1891.

1. Westward—Not Eastward.
2. The Force in Nature—God.
5. The Law of Environment.
6. Benjamin Disraeli.
22. Love as a Corrector.

SERIES V. 1891—1892.

1. Theologies Many—Religion One.
3. Shylock—The Unhistoric Jew.
5. Darkness Before Dawn.
6. On the Threshold.
8. Delusion.
12. Wanted—A Rational Religious School.
14. Civilization's Duty to Woman.
16. Justice, Not Charity.
17. A Personal Interest Society.
18. Ancient and Modern Idolatry.
19. The Law of Retribution.
20. Reverence to Whom Reverence Belongs.
21. Through Labor to Rest.
22. Children's Rights and Parents' Wrongs.
23. Slay the Sin, but Not the Sinner.
24. The Sanctity of the Home.
25. The Noblest Title: "An Honest Man."
26. The Highest Fame: "A Good Name."
27. A Plea for Noble Ambition.

SERIES VI. 1892—1893.

1. Israel's Debt to the New World.
2. Past and Present Purpose of the Church.
3. Ernest Renan.
4. From Doubt to Trust.
5. Sinai and Olympus.
6. One to Sow, Another to Reap.
7. Brethren at Strife.
8. Jew Responsible for Jew
10. Did the Other Prophets Prophecy Jesus?
11. Model Dwellings for the Poor.
12. Under the Lash.
13. The Lost Chord.
14. Sabbath for Man, Not Man for Sabbath.
15. Give While You Live.
16. The Bubble of Glory.
17. Compulsory School Attendance.
19. A Plea for Home Rule in Ireland.
22. To-day.
24. The Red, White and Blue.

SERIES VII. 1893—1894.

1. Religions Die—Religion Lives.
7. Social and Religious Barriers.
11. Debt to Ancestry—Duty to Posterity.
17. A Father's Love.
23. A Sister's and Brother's Love.

SERIES VIII. 1894—1895.

2. My Creed.
4. How Not to Help the Poor.
6. The Stage as a Pulpit.
8. The Pulpit as a Stage.
10. Religion in the Public Schools.
12. "Hope Deferred Maketh the Heart Sick."
16. Post Mortem Praise.
18. The Better for Our Enemies.
20. The Worse for Our Friends.
28. The Israelite as a Husbandman.
31. Arms Against a Sea of Troubles.

SERIES IX. 1895—1896.

2. Ethics or Religion?
3. Faith With Reason.
5. Wherein Israel has Failed.
11. The Place of Prayer in the Service.
13. The Place of Music in the Service.
15. The Place of Ceremony in the Service.

SERIES X. 1896—1897.

2. The Guard Neither Dies nor Surrenders.
4. Thy People Shall be My People.
6. Whoso Tilleth His Soil Shall Have Bread.
8. The Mote and the Beam.
10. What Has Been Shall be Again.
12. The People Without a Country.
13. Uses and Abuses of the Pulpit.
15. Uses and Abuses of the Press.
17. Uses and Abuses of the Novel.
21. The Best Preacher—The Heart.
23. The Best Teacher—Time.
25. The Best Book—The World.
27. The Best Friend—God.
28. Ten Seasons of Sunday Lectures.

SERIES XI. 1897—1898.

1. A Wise Question is the Half of Knowledge.
3. Woe, if All Men Speak Well of You.
5. Good to be Great, Great to be Good.
7. Who is God that I Should Hear Him?
9. Noble Impulses are Speechless Prophets.
18. The Martyr Race.

SERIES XII. 1898—1899.

4. The Gospel of Joy.
6. The Gospel of Sorrow.
10. The Sunset of Life.
12. Old Memories and New Hopes.
18. 90th Birthday of Lincoln and Darwin.
20. The Voice that Calleth in the Wilderness.
21. Turning Parent and Child Toward Each Other.
24. Israel Weak, and Yet Strong.
26. Cyrano de Bergerac, the Story of the Jew.
28. Responsibility of the Rich.

SERIES XIII. 1899—1900.

1. "The Choir Invisible."
9. Chanukah Lights and the Christmas Tree.
12. The Will and the Way.
14. Individual Morality.
16. Domestic Morality.
18. Social Morality.
20. Sectarian Morality.
26. International Morality.
28. Isaac M. Wise—A Memorial Tribute.

SERIES XIV. 1900—1901.

2. From Better to Best.
6. Our Wrongs to Our Little Ones.
8. "We Jews."
10. The Diagnosis.
12. A Remedy.
25. A Time to Keep Silence.
26. "God's First Temples."
27. Daybreak.

Publications of Rabbi Joseph Krauskopf, D. D.

Lincoln, the Chosen of God.

A Discourse, at Temple Keneseth Israel,

BY

Rabbi Joseph Krauskopf, D. D.

Philadelphia, February 11th, 1906.

It was on February 11th, 1861, forty-five years ago this day, that Abraham Lincoln left Springfield, Illinois, to proceed towards the capital of the Nation, as its chosen President. His friends and neighbors came to take leave of him, and, while their hearts rejoiced *Lincoln, on leaving home, asks for prayers.* at the honor that had been conferred upon their fellow-townsman, there were tears in the eyes of many in the hour of parting. Lincoln himself was deeply touched. Had he and they a presentiment that they might never see each other again? "Friends," said he in solemn farewell: "I know not how soon I shall see you again. A duty has devolved upon me greater than that which has devolved upon any other man since Washington. He never would have succeeded except for the aid of Divine Providence, upon which he at all times relied. On the same Almighty Being I place my reliance. Pray that I may receive that Divine assistance, without which I cannot succeed, but with which success is assured."

I have no doubt but that the prayers thus asked for were fervently lifted up for the President elect, and not by his townspeople alone but also by millions of his supporters *Their having been answered questioned.* throughout the troubled land. Was their prayer answered? Many there are who will at once say *no*, and, in proof, will point to a whole Nation inconsolable, aye, to a civilized world in tears, because of his death of martyrdom, a little more than four years after his leave-taking at Springfield.

As for me, I know of no better instance of prayer answered than the success that attended the supplications that were offered up for Lincoln when he entered upon his perilous office. He did not ask that *By reason of his martyrdom.* supplications be offered for his escape from a death of martyrdom; he but asked for prayers that success might attend his labors to save the country from dismemberment and to remove a malignant cancer that threatened the very life of the Nation. In a little more than four years, the Union was saved and slavery was abolished, and, his work being done, the greatest since the days of Washington, martyrdom came as a halo of glory rather than as a sign of failure or as a token of divine disapprobation.

Of course, had mortals had the disposition of it, they would have assigned a far different end to the savior of his

Man would have assigned a different end. Nation and to the emancipator of the slave than death by an assassin's bullet, five short days after General Lee's surrender at Appomattox, on the very day of the rehoisting of Old Glory over Fort Sumter, and but a little more than a month after a grateful people had entrusted itself to his wise and fearless leadership for another term of four years. They would have had him live to a good, old age, they would have had him continue in the full enjoyment of the fruitage of his labors, the idol of his people, the inspiration of all living kind, until a gentle death would have translated him from his field of earthly labor to the regions of his celestial rewards.

But God's ways are not our ways, says the prophet, neither are His thoughts our thoughts. When I consider the

Martyrdom probably design of God. wisdom that was manifest in the choice of this peerless leader, I cannot but feel that in his tragic taking-off, when his work was done, there may have been a wisdom no less divine than that which called him when his work was needed. Probably his highest reward lay in having been spared the ingratitude of the Nation he had saved. Many a savior might have died happy had he died when his work was done, had he died before adulation could turn to envy and envy to malice, and malice to calumny, and calumny to base ingratitude.

Every move in this wonderful man's career seems to speak of providential call and guidance. No man was ever more

No man ever more the chosen of God. the chosen of God than was Abraham Lincoln, and yet no man ever gave less evidence and promise of it than he. What people, unaided by divine direction, would have dared to select for its leader this untried man of the untrained West, in the crisis in which our

Nation found itself prior to the outbreak of the civil war? They would have sought among experienced statesmen, among men of proven executive power, of tried leadership, of great military prowess. They would have inquired among the Universities for those of marked attainments and of brilliant records, or among the illustrious families for one whose distinguished name and descent might dazzle the masses and command the largest following of the select. Only the intermixture of the will of Providence with the will of man can explain the daring choice our fathers made when they selected Abraham Lincoln for their chief-executive. The capitol of Washington had never before, and has never since, seen a President like him. Never before had a man received so little training for so exalted a place, never had a man possessed such few graces for a position that was to throw him in contact with the most polished of the land, never had a man had so little schooling for an office that required profound knowledge in many of the most intricate problems of political and economic and military science.

And never before nor since did man master such gigantic problems, within so short a time, as they were mastered by the first of our martyr-presidents. Long before his first term expired, there was no statesman in all the land comparable to him, no master of the *Never a career like his.* English tongue superior to him, no military strategist like unto the chief-commander of the Nation. Read his deliberations with his cabinet, read his consecration of the battlefield of Gettysburg, his second inaugural address, his orders to his generals, or, better, retrace your steps to the wretched log-cabin in the mountain-wilds of Kentucky, where his cradle stood, and then follow his career, step by step, from cabin to capitol, and tell of another like it, in history or in literature, in fiction or in truth.

His father a backwoodsman, unlettered, unmannered, thriftless. His mother an invalid passing into the grave before her boy is yet nine years old. We next see him in the new lands of Indiana but in the *From cabin to capitol.* midst of the old hardships, differing only from the other in finding here some opportunity for schooling, seven months long in all—the only schooling in all his life. But, if of the school of letters he had little, he had an abundance of the school of life. Life for him, from earliest childhood to manhood's estate, meant hard toil, from early morn till late at night, for little more than the absolute necessities of life. And full of hard toil his life continued to be till his last day, now as farm hand, now as rail-splitter, now as flatboatman, as shopkeeper, soldier, legislator, lawyer, congressman, and finally as President of the United States.

And while that passage from log-cabin to White House, from farmhand to President was marked by wonderful flashes of intellectual genius and of moral and spiritual greatness, such revelations were vouchsafed only to friends and neighbors or to clients and constituents. To the Eastern and Southern people from among whom the Presidents and great men had hitherto come, when they first beheld him, he seemed a gnarled, homely-featured, horn-handed, hoosier from the uncultured West, more fit to drive a yoke of oxen than to guide a nation out of a sea of trouble into a haven of rest.

His fitness at first unrecognized.

Listen to the impression his appearance made on our own townsman, Mr. Alexander McClure, who had done much toward effecting his election, and who had proceeded to Springfield to confer with him on matters of national importance. "My first sight of him was a deep disappointment. Before me stood a middle-aged man, tall, gaunt, ungainly, homely, ill-clad—slouchy pantaloons, vest held shut by a button or two, tightly fitting sleeves to exaggerate his long, bony arms, all supplemented by an awkwardness that was uncommon among men of intelligence. I confess that my heart sank within me as I remembered that this was the man chosen by a great nation to become its ruler in the gravest period of its history."

Even by his friends

It was not long, however, before Mr. McClure discovered, as the Nation discovered later, that it was God who had chosen Lincoln, that, when the people cast their vote for him, they but expressed the will of Providence, which had decreed that the Nation founded by the Colonial Fathers shall not be severed, and that the slave shall be free. They remembered what the Bible said respecting the choice of the shepherd David in preference of other

His divine call made manifest at last.

men, who, in external appearance, seemed the better fitted for the kingship: "the Lord seeth not as man seeth; for man looketh on the outward appearance, but the Lord looketh on the heart." They recalled the humble origin of Moses and Jesus and Luther, and recognized that they whom God chooses for his work must have other distinctions than looks or wealth or name or culture. They must have hearts of saints, souls of heroes and martyrs. They must serve as anvils in the smithies of affliction so as to be able to serve as the hammer of God when the hour for striking comes.

It was a critical time in the story of our Nation, the most critical since the days of our conflict with our mother country across the sea. The hand of brother was lifted against brother. The South stood arrayed against _{In the need of the hour.} the North. The hour called for a great man, for a man wise of heart as well as of mind, for a man of inspired soul and resolute will, for a man whose personal ties and family traditions counted as nothing in the balance, for a man who, being of the common people, and the conflict of the hour having the greatest need of the common people, could easiest appeal to them and come in closest touch with them. The hour called for a man all whose labor and ambition were consecrated to his people and all whose purposes accountable to his God.

Such a man was Lincoln. A man more honest than he never lived. Rivals derided him, parties ridiculed him, papers carricatured him but no man was ever able even to breathe the breath of suspicion upon any of _{The heart of a saint.} his motives. Unlike so many of the schooled diplomats and statesmen, who, in their eager development of brain, starve the heart, his brain was all the keener because of its blending with heart, and his heart all the richer because of its blending with brain. An unkind word never passed his lips, an unkind deed never stained his hand, an unworthy thought never polluted his mind. His countenance, rugged and gnarled as it was, was as open as a page of Scriptures; his eye as clear as innocence itself.

Not ambition, not lust of power or wealth, of fame or name, bore him to the heights he occupied. He had never sought an honor or an office, had never thought himself fit for a position of responsibility when it was entrusted to him.

Men in public office have been modest, have been unassuming, but never one like Abraham Lincoln. There was no more surprised man in all the land than he was when the choice of President fell to him, and it would have been difficult to find one who could have accepted it with greater reluctance. Full forty years long had he yearned for the coming of a man strong and wise enough to rid the Nation of the curse of slavery, without severing its bond of union. Full forty years long had that hope and prayer burnt within him, and would not cease burning, like the vision of the burning bush that Moses saw in the wilderness. And when the call came to him at last, as it had come to Moses, when the voice of God, through the voice of the people, called out to him, saying: "I have seen the afflictions of a people unjustly enslaved; I have heard its cry of anguish by reason of its taskmasters. I know the strife that is tearing the Nation asunder, and I am resolved to deliver it, through thy hand. Get thee to Washington, and inaugurate there the work of redemption and of union," when that call came, he, like Moses, had not the heart to rush upon a work, which the greatest had feared to touch, fearing lest, by unfitness, he overthrow all future chance, all further hope. "Let another and an abler go," he sadly said, "this is a work for giants, not for pigmies, like me."

It was a work for a giant, and for just such a giant as Lincoln was. It required a giant's heart to make an entry into the capital of the Nation, as President elect, **The soul of a hero.** such as he was obliged to make, in the dead of night, by stealth and by circuitous routes, to escape the assassin's hand. It required a giant's mind to present an inaugural address such as he presented, on the fourth of March, 1861, and to outline a course of action such as he laid before his Secretary of State. The men of his cabinet, proud of their statesmanship and scholarship and polish and influence, had believed that the Western hoosier, the accident of the polls, would but be a figurehead, that they themselves would rule and dictate the policies of the land. They soon learned that their chief was a ruler, not only by the grace but also by the call of God, a ruler with the inspiration of a prophet, with the wisdom of a sage, with the will-power of a conqueror. Before a month of his presidential term had elapsed, the Nation marvelled as much as it had doubted, and the South realized that it was a war to the death that it had entered upon.

And a war to the death it continued, four years long, till slavery was abolished and the union was saved. There was no abatement in its vigor, no change in its policy, no quarter to the enemy, until they recognized the stars and stripes as the common flag of all of the United States, until they conceded to the enslaved negro the human rights and political liberties which the white man enjoyed. There had been irresoluteness and vacillation too long, and at too terrible a cost. Had the issue been squarely met, had the voice of God instead of the voice of politics been spoken, had there been whole truths instead of half measures, in short, had there been a Lincoln in the Presidential chair fifty years earlier, there would have been no need of a civil war, no need of ravaged states, devastated homes, paralyzed industries, impoverished people, no need of brother's hand being raised against brother, no need of six hundred and twenty-five battles being fought, in which blood flowed like water, and which widowed and orphaned and darkened tens of thousands of homes.

His purpose immovable.

Others before him had seen the calamity that threatened the Nation as clearly as he saw it, and had yearned for a redeemer as sincerely as he. Long before him, Patrick Henry had said the slave question "gives a gloomy prospect to future times," and George Mason had written to the legislature of Virginia "the laws of impartial Providence may avenge our injustice upon our posterity," and Jefferson had said: "I tremble for my country when I reflect that God is just, and that His justice cannot sleep for ever," and Madison had said "where slavery exists there the republican theory becomes fallacious,"—but, while they saw the danger and despaired, he felt it and acted.

Others dared not to risk their political future.

Others dared not to risk their political future, he dared to risk even his life. It was his innermost conviction that one nation, under one government, without slavery, had been divinely ordained, and he was resolved that not a State should be struck from the union by treason. He saw no other assurance for lasting peace than war to the bitter end, no other promise of harmony between

He dared to risk his life.

the North and South than a decision upon the battlefield
whether or not all men are born free and equal politically,
whether or not individual states had a right to secede. It was
in our old Independence Hall where he solemnly declared that
he believed in the Declaration of Independence, that he believed
with all his heart that it guaranteed liberty to all, and reaching
a climax of eloquence, and speaking as one inspired, he said:
"If the country cannot be saved without giving up that
principle, I would rather be assassinated on the spot than
surrender it."

And well did he see to it that the country did not surrender
its principle. And dearly did he pay for it. That of which
he had had a presentiment when he spoke in our
city came to pass. The assassin's hand struck

*And paid it to the
assassin.*

him down, but not till, by his labors, his country
was saved, till the stars and stripes waved again over the North
and South, till union and federal soldier laid down their arms,
never to take them up again against each other.

The turf has grown thick over the graves of those who
paid with their lives for their country's honor. The bitter
enmities of half a century ago are now forgotten.
But not forgotten is the name of Abraham Lincoln. Not forgotten is the sacrifice of martyrdom
which he laid upon the altar of his country.

*Lives immortal as
Savior of the union
as Freer of the
slave.*

Annually the still remaining veterans of the long and deadly
conflict assemble to do reverence to the memory of their well-
nigh canonized leader. Annually sons of these veterans assemble
to pledge their fealty to the memory of him who led their
fathers and their country to victory. Annually, on his natal
day, a grateful posterity burnishes into new lustre his crown
of glory, and piously resolves that as long as oceans shall
beat against our Atlantic and Pacific shores, as long as the
Alleghenies and the Rocky Mountains shall lift their heads
into the blue empyrean, as long as proud Old Glory shall wave
from highest North to furthest South, so long shall the name
of Abraham Lincoln live in the loyal American heart as the
savior of his country, as the Chosen of God.

Ready in Bookform

The Eighteenth Series of
Sunday Discourses of . . .
Rabbi Jos. Krauskopf, D. D.

Price $1.50.   Address

OSCAR KLONOWER,

1435 Euclid Avenue, Philadelphia.

THE Series of Discourses delivered by Rabbi Joseph Krauskopf,
D. D., at the Temple Keneseth Israel, Philadelphia, entitled

"Some Isms of To-day"

I.—EGOISM,
II.—ALTRUISM,
III.—PESSIMISM,
IV.—OPTIMISM,
V.—REALISM,
VI.—IDEALISM,
VII.—DOWIEISM,
VIII.—MYSTICISM,
IX.—TRADE-UNIONISM,

in **Bookform**, handsomely bound, with a new Steel Engraving of the Author.   Price $1.00.

OSCAR KLONOWER,
1435 Euclid Avenue,   Philadelphia.